BEI GRIN MACHT SICH IHR WISSEN BEZAHLT

AF138454

- Wir veröffentlichen Ihre Hausarbeit, Bachelor- und Masterarbeit

- Ihr eigenes eBook und Buch - weltweit in allen wichtigen Shops

- Verdienen Sie an jedem Verkauf

Jetzt bei www.GRIN.com hochladen und kostenlos publizieren

GRIN

Floating Waste Identification in Water Bodies with an AI-Driven Boat System

Punugoti Venkatesh

Bibliografische Information der Deutschen Nationalbibliothek:

Die Deutsche Nationalbibliothek verzeichnet diese Publikation in der Deutschen Nationalbibliografie; detaillierte bibliografische Daten sind im Internet über http://dnb.d-nb.de abrufbar.

ISBN: 9783346906540
Dieses Buch ist auch als E-Book erhältlich.

Druck und Bindung: Books on Demand GmbH, Norderstedt Germany
Gedruckt auf säurefreiem Papier aus verantwortungsvollen Quellen

Das vorliegende Werk wurde sorgfältig erarbeitet. Dennoch übernehmen Autoren und Verlag für die Richtigkeit von Angaben, Hinweisen, Links und Ratschlägen sowie eventuelle Druckfehler keine Haftung.

Das Buch bei GRIN: https://www.grin.com/document/1370950

FLOATING WASTE IDENTIFICATION IN WATERBODIES
(SMART-BOAT)

A DTM 002 PROJECT REPORT

Submitted by
P VENKATESH

In partial fulfilment for the award of the degree of

BACHELOR OF TECHNOLOGY
In
COMPUTER SCIENCE ENGINEERING & MECHANICAL ENGINEERING

ALLIANCE COLLEGE OF ENGINEERING AND DESIGN

ALLIANCE UNIVERSITY, BENGALURU

JANUARY- 2023

ACKNOWLEDGEMENT

The satisfaction derived from successfully completing a task would be incomplete without acknowledging the individuals who contributed to its accomplishment. I am immensely grateful to my supervisors, **Dr. Lokesh Singh, Dr. V Keerthika, and Prof. Asha Rani NR**, for their unwavering guidance and support throughout the project. Their wise counsel and valuable suggestions have been indispensable.

I would like to express my thanks to **Dr. Abhram Gorge**, Head of the Department (CSE), **Dr. Girish BM**, Head of Department (ME), and **Dr. Reeba Korah**, Dean, for their encouragement and cooperation at various stages of the project.

I am particularly grateful to **Dr. Lokesh Singh**, Associate Professor and DTM Coordinator of Alliance College of Engineering and Design.

I would also like to extend my sincere appreciation to the management of Alliance University for providing exceptional infrastructure, a conducive environment, and continuous support.

My heartfelt gratitude goes to the teaching and non-teaching staff of our department, who stood by me throughout the project and contributed to its success.

Lastly, I hold my parents, friends, and well-wishers in the highest regard for their invaluable assistance in preparing the report of this project.

P VENKATESH

ABSTRACT

Today, water is being contaminated at a higher rate which increases the pollution level. Water in ponds is not being maintained as it is not a major concern. Also, the floating waste in the ponds are increasing due to ignorance. The current methods of organic and non-organic waste removal from water bodies are inefficient, labour-intensive, and lack precise waste segregation techniques. This leads to environmental degradation, contamination of aquatic ecosystems, and poses a threat to biodiversity and human health.

Therefore, there is a pressing need to develop an AI-driven boat system that can autonomously and effectively remove, segregate, and dispose of both organic and non-organic waste, improving waste management practices in water bodies.

In this system, Image processing techniques can be employed to detect the floating wastes (organic and non-organic) and removal of waste can be done with suitable sensors. The information regarding the waste and pH level are stored in cloud periodically and so it can be accessed through IoT. Since the information is stored in cloud the co-ordinates of the boat can be obtained for proper maintenance of the smart boat

CONTENTS

1.INTRODUCTION

Water is contaminated at a larger scale due to disposal of plastic wastes in the water. It pollutes the waterbodies which is harmful to the aquatic organisms and for the consumers. Removal of that plastic wastes is necessary to increase the purity level of the water. Water pollution caused by organic and non-organic waste poses a significant threat to aquatic ecosystems, human health, and biodiversity.

Traditional methods of waste removal are often time-consuming, labour-intensive, and less effective in handling large-scale pollution. An AI-driven boat designed specifically for the removal of both organic and non-organic waste from water bodies. The integration of artificial intelligence (AI) technologies into a boat enables efficient waste collection, segregation, and disposal, contributing to environmental sustainability and pH level monitoring is also an important factor to measure the purity content of water.

Object detection is a complex undertaking in the field of computer vision. It presents numerous challenges due to the wide range of variations in orientation, lighting conditions, backgrounds, and occlusion that can be recognized as different images instead of the real image. This project is to create a real-time object detection and identification algorithm with the use of image acquisition and processing technique.

2 LITERATURE SURVEY

As a part of literature survey some of the product that already exists in the market were reviewed. The aim is to observe how these applications work and to see how they can be improved and how different they are. To date it is identified that the following products are offering relatively similar service.

1. **Solar Breeze NX2:** The Solar Breeze NX2 is a solar-powered robotic pool skimmer that can also be used in ponds. It operates using solar energy and has a large debris collection tray to gather leaves, pollen, and other floating debris. It navigates the pond using a combination of sensors and paddle wheels.[2]

2. **Oase AquaActiv PondJet Floating Fountain and Pond Cleaner:** The Oase AquaActiv PondJet is a multifunctional device that combines a floating fountain with pond cleaning capabilities. It has an integrated suction function that removes debris from the pond's surface. The collected debris is then collected in a filter bag. The PondJet also offers adjustable fountain heights and patterns for aesthetic appeal.[1]

3. **Laguna Power Clean Cordless Pond Cleaner:** The Laguna Power Clean is a cordless pond cleaner that operates on rechargeable batteries. It uses a suction mechanism to remove debris, leaves, and other pollutants from the pond. The cleaner comes with a telescopic pole for easy manoeuvrability and a collection bag to store the debris.[4]

4. **Robotek Lagoon Cleaning Robot:** The Robotek Lagoon Cleaning Robot is an autonomous boat designed specifically for pond and lake cleaning. It uses GPS and obstacle detection sensors to navigate and clean the water surface effectively. The robot is equipped with brushes and a debris collection system, and it can be programmed to clean specific areas of the pond.[3]

2.1 USER SURVEY

A questionnaire was circulated via Google Forms as a way of understanding the perception of users and to give the inside view of the smart boat

Are you aware of the waste and debris pollution in ponds can affect the aquatic life.
102 responses

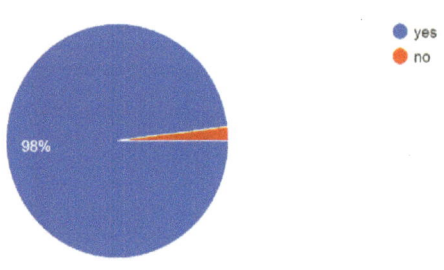

How important do you think it is to address waste pollution in ponds?
102 responses

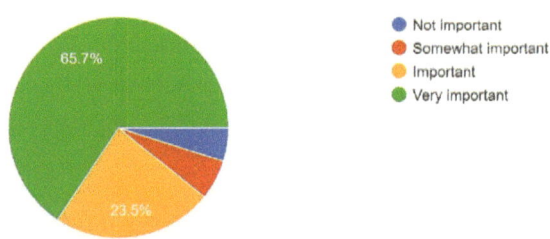

Would you support the use of a smart boat for waste collection in ponds?

102 responses

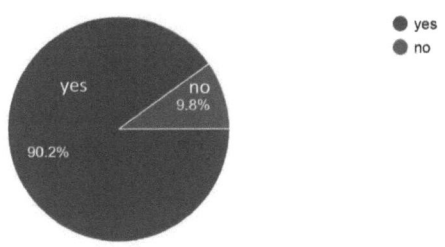

- yes
- no

yes 90.2%

no 9.8%

How do you envision the smart boat being operated? Should it be manually controlled by an operator or have autonomous capabilities?

102 responses

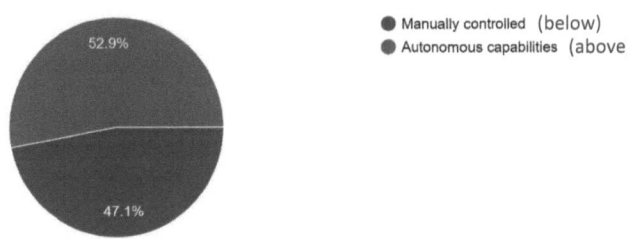

- Manually controlled (below)
- Autonomous capabilities (above)

52.9%

47.1%

What features do you think a smart boat for waste collection should have? (Multiple choice: Select all that apply)

102 responses

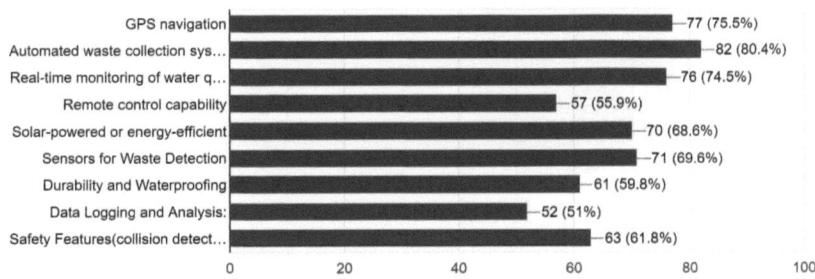

GPS navigation	77 (75.5%)
Automated waste collection sys...	82 (80.4%)
Real-time monitoring of water q...	76 (74.5%)
Remote control capability	57 (55.9%)
Solar-powered or energy-efficient	70 (68.6%)
Sensors for Waste Detection	71 (69.6%)
Durability and Waterproofing	61 (59.8%)
Data Logging and Analysis:	52 (51%)
Safety Features(collision detect...	63 (61.8%)

How would you rate the current efforts by government or organizations to tackle waste pollution in water bodies?(1-poor & 5-best)
102 responses

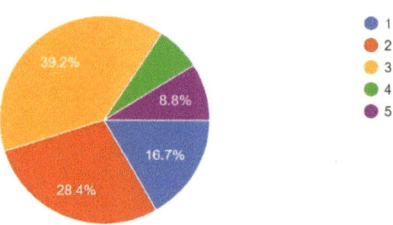

- 1
- 2
- 3
- 4
- 5

What is your expected battery life for a smart boat with image detection and automatic waste collection?
102 responses

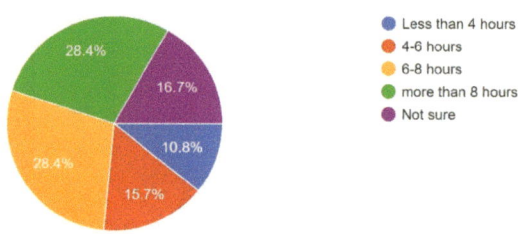

- Less than 4 hours
- 4-6 hours
- 6-8 hours
- more than 8 hours
- Not sure

Have you ever seen a boat that has technology to classify and clean waste itself?
102 responses

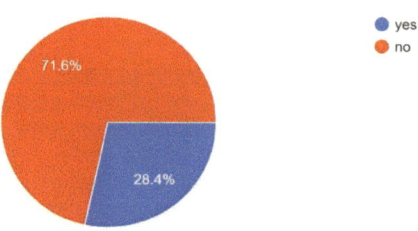

- yes
- no

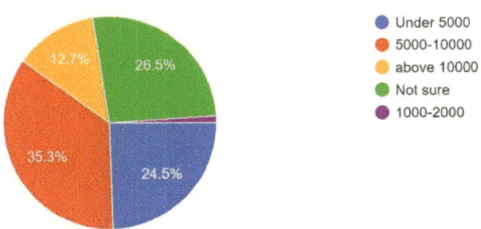

How much would you be willing to pay for a high-quality smart BOAT?(in INR)

102 responses

- Under 5000
- 5000-10000
- above 10000
- Not sure
- 1000-2000

2.2SUMMARY FOR USER SURVEY

- As per the user survey we have noticed that majority of the users have agreed that waste and debris accumulation in ponds is major issue to the aquatic life and the environment itself.
- It was also notice that the large scale of users were aware of this problem.
- A majority of the users have also supported our "smart boat" project for the waste collection.

Considering the reviews of the users we will try implementing the following features:

- The smart boat will be fully automatic.
- Implementation of GPS and water quality testing.
- Waste collection will also be fully automatic.
- The battery life will be extended to 6-8 hours.
- Fully functionable on solar energy.

Apart from the features we have notices that:

- The budget of the boat will made around 5k-10k (INR).
- Users are not satisfied with the current progress of the government and
- They haven't seen any technology like our "smart boat" which is currently working.

3.PROBLEM STATEMENT

It is estimated that according to reports, over 22 million pounds of plastic pollution find their way into the Great Lakes each year. recent research conducted in "Rochester Institute of Technology" and is a persistent problem that does not disappear over time. As well as the floating waste in the ponds are increasing due to ignorance which affects the purity of water. Plastic wastes in lakes can cause a range of environmental problems, including:

- Water pollution
- Harm to wildlife
- Damage to habitats
- Human health risks

And because of Eichhornia which causes obstruction of water transportation, and fishing activities and clogging of the water ways which causes reduction of water quality.

3.1 NEED FOR THE PROJECT

To make the system smarter, data is directly fed to cloud which can be accessed further. By continuous monitoring of waste using image processing technology, removal can be done immediately. In case of immersing or missing of boat, location can be identified through GPS.

3.2 4W FRAMEWORK

- Who: Local people around the lake
- What: Pollution of lake
- Where: Contamination of plastic waste
- Why: To make the water clean and usable

4.OBJECTIVE OF THE PROJECT

The objective of the smart boat can vary from use to use. Some of them can be:

- **Autonomous Operation:** The primary objective of a smart boat is to operate autonomously, without the need for constant human intervention. It should be able to navigate the pond, detect obstacles, and clean the water surface effectively, all while making independent decisions based on its programmed algorithms and sensor inputs.

- **Efficient Debris Removal:** A smart boat aims to efficiently and effectively remove debris, leaves, algae, and other pollutants from the pond's surface. It should have the capability to collect and store the debris for easy disposal or subsequent treatment, ensuring a clean and debris-free water surface.

- **Water Quality Maintenance:** The smart boat should contribute to maintaining and improving water quality in the pond. It may incorporate features such as water filtration, skimming mechanisms, or chemical dosing systems to remove impurities and maintain optimal water conditions for aquatic life.

- **Navigation and Obstacle Avoidance:** An important objective is to enable the smart boat to navigate the pond autonomously while avoiding obstacles. This requires robust sensor systems, including GPS or RTK for accurate positioning, as well as obstacle detection sensors to detect and avoid potential hazards such as rocks, floating objects, or shallow areas.

- **User-Friendly Interface:** The smart boat should be equipped with a user-friendly interface that enables effortless control, monitoring, and adjustment of its cleaning parameters. This can be achieved through features like remote-control capability, smartphone applications, or intuitive control panels, ensuring a smooth and convenient user experience.

- **Versatility and Adaptability:** Smart boats may aim to be versatile and adaptable to different pond sizes, shapes, and conditions. They should be capable of adjusting their cleaning patterns, speed, or depth to accommodate various types of ponds and efficiently clean different areas within the water body.

- **Energy Efficiency:** Smart boats may strive to be energy-efficient by incorporating renewable energy sources such as solar power or utilizing efficient propulsion systems.

This objective aims to reduce energy consumption and promote environmentally friendly operation.

5.PROJECT PLAN

Water is being contaminated at a higher rate which increases the pollution level. Water in ponds is not being maintained as it is not a major concern. As well as the floating waste (Organic and inorganic) in the ponds are increasing due to ignorance. So, necessary measures must be undertaken in order to maintain purity of water. In this system, with the help of Arduino uno module, the floating wastes are detected and identified using Image processing technique and the boat will be attach with a carrier in the front to carry all the waste and shaft/blades which will cut all the underneath plant which comes in the way to obstruct the smooth flow of the boat. Motors is used to move the boat forward. Simultaneously, the purity of the water is also identified with the help of pH sensors. The location of the boat can also be identified using GPS which will show the exact location of the boat in case if it requires any external manpower. The information regarding the wastes, GPS co-ordinates and pH level can be viewed in webpage.

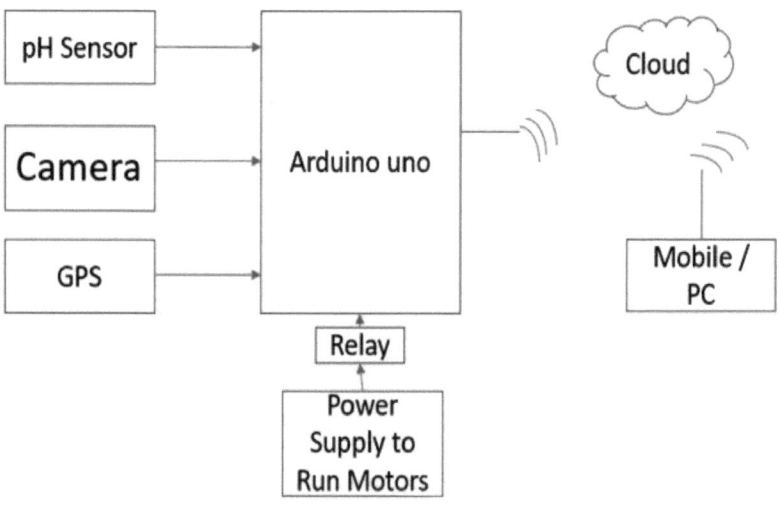

5.1 DESIGN OF THE PROJECT

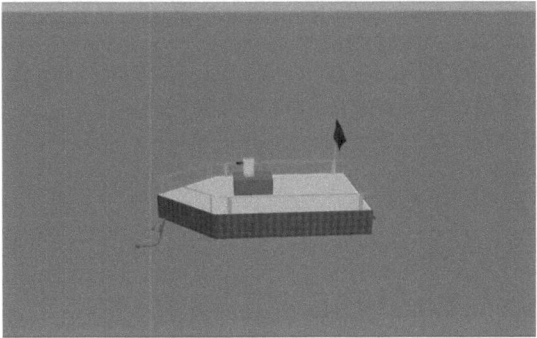

Fig:1.1[side view]

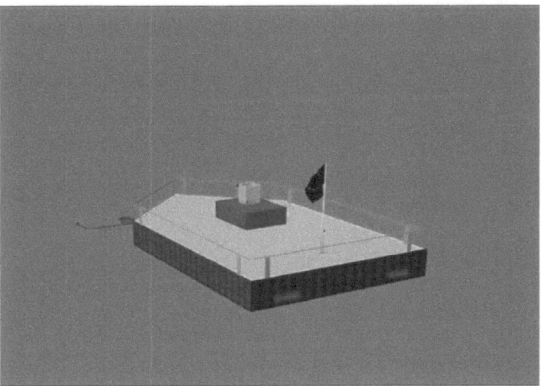

Fig:1.2[arial view]

The basic design of the boat will be kind of as shown above. It will be having pair of motors for the movement, a camera to capture the images, a carrier and blade for the collection and removal of debris and plastic waste from the water bodies.

5.2 CODE

```
import os
import time      import cv2 import numpy as np import pandas as pd import tensorflow as tf
import  matplotlib.pyplot  as  plt  from  PIL  import  Image,  ImageOps  from
tensorflow.keras.models import Sequential from tensorflow.keras.layers import Dense, Flatten,
Conv2D, MaxPooling2D, Dropout, BatchNormalization from tensorflow.keras.callbacks
import EarlyStopping, ModelCheckpoint, ReduceLROnPlateau
from tensorflow.keras.preprocessing.image import ImageDataGenerator

# Ignore the warning. import
warnings
warnings.filterwarnings('ignore'
)
#---------------------------------------- notebook_start_time
= time.time()

img_train_path        =        os.path.join("/kaggle/input/waste-
classificationdata/","DATASET","TRAIN")
img_test_path = os.path.join("/kaggle/input/waste-classification-data/","DATASET","TEST")
data_gen   =   ImageDataGenerator(rescale=1./255,   fill_mode='reflect')   val_gen   =
ImageDataGenerator(rescale=1./255)

train_gen        =        data_gen.flow_from_directory(img_train_path,
target_size=(256,256), batch_size=128)
validation_gen        =        val_gen.flow_from_directory(img_test_path,
target_size=(256,256), batch_size=128)

img_train_path        =        os.path.join("/kaggle/input/waste-
classificationdata/","DATASET","TRAIN")
img_test_path = os.path.join("/kaggle/input/waste-classification-data/","DATASET","TEST")
data_gen   =   ImageDataGenerator(rescale=1./255,   fill_mode='reflect')   val_gen   =
ImageDataGenerator(rescale=1./255)

train_gen        =        data_gen.flow_from_directory(img_train_path,
target_size=(256,256), batch_size=128)
validation_gen        =        val_gen.flow_from_directory(img_test_path,
target_size=(256,256), batch_size=128)

print("Train/Validation indicies: ", train_gen.class_indices)
print("\n0 Stands for Organic \"O\", and 1 stands for Non-Organic \"R\"")

img, _ = next(train_gen)
```

```python
plt.figure(figsize=(15, 13))

for i in range(30):    ax =
plt.subplot(6, 6, i + 1)
plt.imshow(img[i])    if
_[i][1] == 0:
    plt.title("Organic")
else:
    plt.title("Non-Organic")
plt.axis("off") del img
del _

model = tf.keras.Sequential()

# Add convolutional layers
model.add(tf.keras.layers.Conv2D(32,(3,3), activation='relu', input_shape=(256, 256, 3)))
model.add(tf.keras.layers.MaxPooling2D(pool_size=(2,                                    2)))
model.add(tf.keras.layers.Conv2D(64,        (3,        3),        activation='relu'))
model.add(tf.keras.layers.MaxPooling2D(pool_size=(2,                                    2)))
model.add(tf.keras.layers.Conv2D(128,       (3,        3),        activation='relu'))
model.add(tf.keras.layers.MaxPooling2D(pool_size=(2,                                    2)))
model.add(tf.keras.layers.Conv2D(256,       (3,        3),        activation='relu'))
model.add(tf.keras.layers.MaxPooling2D(pool_size=(2, 2)))

# Add fully-connected layers with weight decay model.add(tf.keras.layers.Flatten())
model.add(tf.keras.layers.Dense(256,        activation='relu',
kernel_regularizer=tf.keras.regularizers.L1L2(l2=0.001)))
model.add(tf.keras.layers.Dense(128,        activation='relu',
kernel_regularizer=tf.keras.regularizers.L1L2(l2=0.001))) model.add(tf.keras.layers.Dense(2,
activation='softmax')) model.summary()
model.compile(optimizer='Nadam',loss='CategoricalCrossentropy', metrics=['accuracy'])

early_stopping_monitor      =         EarlyStopping(monitor='val_loss',      patience=5,
restore_best_weights=True)

best_model = ModelCheckpoint('bestmodel.hdf5', monitor='val_loss', save_best_only=True)

history      =      model.fit(train_gen,      validation_data=validation_gen,      epochs=30,
callbacks=[best_model, early_stopping_monitor])
```

```python
plt.figure(figsize=[10,6])
plt.plot(history.history["accuracy"], label = "Train acc")
plt.plot(history.history["val_accuracy"], label = "Validation acc") plt.legend()
plt.show()


plt.figure(figsize=(10,6))
plt.plot(history.history['loss'], label = "Train loss")
plt.plot(history.history['val_loss'], label = "Validation loss")
plt.legend()
plt.show()

model.load_weights('bestmodel.hdf5')
model.evaluate(validation_gen);

def        predict_func(img):
result = model.predict(img)
return result

img, _= next(validation_gen)
plt.figure(figsize=(15,    13))
result = model.predict(img)
for i in range(30):      ax =
plt.subplot(6,   6,   i   +   1)
plt.imshow(img[i])              if
result[i][1] < 0.5:
    pred = 0         if
pred == _[i][1]:
      plt.title("Organic", color='green')
else:          plt.title("Organic",
color='red')    else:
    pred = 1          if
pred == _[i][1]:
      plt.title("Non-Organic",       color='green')
else:
      plt.title("Non-Organic",                color='red')
plt.axis("off")
```

5.3 ARDUINO CODE:

```
const int motorPin1 = 2;    const
int motorPin2 = 3;
const int enablePin = 4;


int motorSpeed = 0;
int motorDirection = 0;

void setup() {

  pinMode(motorPin1,                        OUTPUT);
pinMode(motorPin2, OUTPUT);
  pinMode(enablePin, OUTPUT);


  motorDirection = 1;
motorSpeed    =    0;
stopMotor();
}

void loop() {

  setMotorDirection(1);

  setMotorSpeed(200);
delay(1000);
stopMotor();
delay(1000);
}

void setMotorDirection(int direction) {

  if    (direction    ==    1)    {
digitalWrite(motorPin1,    HIGH);
digitalWrite(motorPin2, LOW);
  }              else                {
digitalWrite(motorPin1, LOW);
  digitalWrite(motorPin2, HIGH);
  }
}
```

```
void setMotorSpeed(int speed) {

  analogWrite(enablePin, speed);
}

void          stopMotor()          {
analogWrite(enablePin, 0);
}
```

5.4 THE RESULT

We will get this kind of output screen for our project:

This figure has been removed for copyright reasons.

Fig:2[classification into organic and inorganic]

With the help of input data set we are expecting to get this kind of output screen. As our images will be classified only into two categories

- Organic: All the waste which are biodegradable comes under this category
- Non-organic: All the waste which cannot degrade come under this category

6 CURRENT STATUS OF PROJECT

As we were successfully able to develop the code for the classification of the image using CNN, and basic software model of the boat was also created. All the basic and important material for the project have been collected. Code for the movement of the boat using Arduino was also successfully executed.

6.1 AREAS TO FOCUS

- Have to club the code for Arduino and image classification into one platform.
- Selection of the proper material for the framework of the boat has to be done.
- Combining all the components carefully.

7 CONTRIBUTIONS

Research and findings	Sandeep,Aravind,Keerthana,Venkatesh
Data set collection	Sandeep
Coding and development	Sandeep, Aravind
debugging	Keerthana, Venkatesh, Sandeep
Modelling of boat	Aravind
Planning the setup and note making	Keerthana, Aravind
User feedback	Sandeep, Venkatesh
Power point presentation	Venkatesh, Keerthana
Material collection	Sandeep
Working on budget	Keerthana, Aravind
Documentation	Sandeep, Keerthana, Aravind, Venkatesh

8 CONCLUSIONS

Firstly, the development of smart boats equipped with advanced sensors, navigation systems, and debris collection mechanisms has demonstrated their potential in efficiently and effectively cleaning ponds. These autonomous systems offer significant time savings and ensure consistent cleaning, contributing to improved water quality and a healthier pond ecosystem.

Secondly, the integration of intelligent algorithms for autonomous navigation, obstacle avoidance, and path planning has proven crucial in the safe and efficient operation of smart boats. These algorithms enable precise maneuvering and effective coverage of the pond, optimizing the cleaning process and reducing the risk of collisions or damage to the boat and its surroundings.

The findings of this project emphasize the significance of smart boats in automating and improving pond cleaning processes. By reducing manual labour, improving efficiency, and enhancing water quality, smart boats offer a sustainable and effective solution for pond maintenance.

Smart boats represent a promising technology that can revolutionize the field of pond cleaning. With continued and innovation, these autonomous systems have the potential to enhance water quality, preserve ecosystems, and contribute to a cleaner and more sustainable environment.

9 REFERENCE

1. **IoT Based Water Surface Cleaning and Quality Checking Boat:** By B. Saran Raj, L. Murali, B. Vijayaparamesh, J. Sharan Kumar and P. Pragadeesh on 2021. Retrieved from https://iopscience.iop.org/article/10.1088/1742-6596/1937/1/012023

2. **Swachh Hasth-A Water Cleaning Robot:** By Siddhanna Janai , H N Supreetha , Bhoomika S , Yogithashree R P, Pallavi M on 2020. Retrieved from https://www.ijert.org/

3. **IoT Based Water Pollution Monitoring RC Boat:** By Mohamed Aslam, Sreerag K, Stebin T Jose, Mr. G. Chandrashekar on 2022. Retrieved from International Journal of Advanced Research in Science, Communication and Technology (IJARSCT)

4. **Remote controlled Aquawaste collector with Iot Based water pollution monitoring and tracking system:** By Rahul Patil, Ranjeet Ghatage, Sagar C Goni, Vineet Sharat Torke, Soumya Halagatti on 2023. Retrieved from international Journal of Research Publication and Reviews.